The Sun, Moon, Mars, and The Stars

Ashwath Narayan

Copyright © Ashwath Narayan 2024
All Rights Reserved.

ISBN 979-8-89186-562-4

This book has been published with all efforts taken to make the material error-free after the consent of the author. However, the author and the publisher do not assume and hereby disclaim any liability to any party for any loss, damage, or disruption caused by errors or omissions, whether such errors or omissions result from negligence, accident, or any other cause.

While every effort has been made to avoid any mistake or omission, this publication is being sold on the condition and understanding that neither the author nor the publishers or printers would be liable in any manner to any person by reason of any mistake or omission in this publication or for any action taken or omitted to be taken or advice rendered or accepted on the basis of this work. For any defect in printing or binding the publishers will be liable only to replace the defective copy by another copy of this work then available.

You said "Perhaps love is curative".
It *was*.

i believed if
i was just perfect i would
then be worth loving

Contents

Act I: Utopia

Contents

Act II: Paradise Lost

Act III: Tomorrow is a Long Time

Act I: Utopia

Share My Heart

I had already given away my whole heart
When I met you at the start
I had nothing left with which to part
You saw this but you didn't depart

That I had dedicated myself
For a furry four-legged elf
For me he had given all of himself
And I loved him more than life itself

We're so similar, he and I
Neglected, abandoned, left to die
Betrayed even by our own body
On our side there was nobody

He chose me on that fateful day
I'll say it was magic if I may
I saw wonder in his eye
I wonder what he saw in I

Sooner than our lives together had begun
We amalgamated, became one
My baby boy, my son
The center of my world, the sun

He cared for me like family
And I for him too, dutifully
We healed each other, just us two
Together the world we stood up to

He gave me more than I could hold
His soul so pure, his spirit gold
The best part of me is he
He's the reason you fell for me

No creature in all the universe
Should have suffered his undeserving curse
So pure, so loving, so good
Mistreated, abused, misunderstood

He wasn't fazed by the negativity
His soul unblackened by calamity
He was, that way, the opposite of me
Even fought off the devil in me

He gave me purpose, a reason to be
Allowed me to care for him so I could see
In this world there was a place for me
Saved me from drowning in misery

Misery that which was a ravaging sea
He swam that ocean and rescued me
He studied my heart like angiography
Told me I wasn't fruit from the poisonous tree

He tricked me with compassionate eyes
For really he's an angel in disguise
Our hearts beat together now, they synchronise
My blessings he made me realise

But in his impossible enterprise
My demons he did internalise
His wings and magic I saw vapourize
I was wretched, but he sacrificed

I'm sure you see
That he's the only good in me
Why he's the priority
Why I fear constantly

So please hear this plea

Share with him this heart in me

For without his magic you will see

Demons, and then how would you love me?

my superpower
was invisibility
how did you see me?

Are You a Vampire Slayer?

I had grown accustomed to the darkness
My shadow held tight like a harness
The days were bleak,
Their coming I did not seek

This battle can never be won
For eternity I'd have to run
For when the night was done
Out came my enemy the sun

A creature of the night
Hiding from the daylight
Like Tolkein's Smegal a dismal sight
My appearance sure to cause fright
No hope in my foresight
Pain was my only delight

Don't look at me with those eyes that pity
Unsure how to disguise sympathy
I'm too proud for charity
Too far gone for clarity
So far from reality
Gripped in insanity

Like a monster of imagination
I began to practise hibernation
I lost all of human sensation
My memories dissolved in fragmentation
My only habit became lamentation

The legends you have heard are true
A Vampire isn't one with to rendezvous
He will tear your spirit from your tissue
He will drink your soul like it is stew
He will destroy all that is you

This is a hell of my own creation
Unlikely is my salvation
Aren't you afraid of my incarnation?
Haven't you heard of my reputation?
You won't escape this hallucination
Prepare for your certain incarceration

How is it that you are free?
My magic is of the highest degree
Enslaved and subdued you should be
What is this power in thee?
Alas, you will exorcise me!

Did You Get Botched Eye Surgery?

When I was invisible
A shadow in the dark
Living beneath a rock
Nothing more than a misplaced sock
You saw me

You saw my dry skin and coarse hair
My racoon eyes and soul bare
My brittle bones, hard overtones
My body like a corpse emaciated
If I was you I would have apparated

You saw me
When I looked and felt like death
Without passion or dreams like Macbeth
Detached from the world, shibboleth

You saw me
When I couldn't get myself out of bed
Or recognise the memories in my head
So many of them tained blood-red
To escape these ghosts I'd softly tread

I was nothing but a shell

A fish drowning in a dry well

I'm as concerned as I am grateful

For what followed was fateful

But tell me, back then what did you see?

Surely you've had botched eye surgery!

Am I Dreaming?

The swallows swooped through the canopy
Their mating ritual displayed for all to see
An act that seemed too private for my eyes
But they were unbothered in the skies

As the red sun disappeared beneath the horizon
And the blood-orange sky pulled our eyes in
The blue butterflies made the most of the daylight
As it faded away into the twilight

The leaves danced in the breeze
The crisp wind for a brief moment a freeze
I saw the smile widen on your pretty face
I pulled you indoors for the warmth of your embrace

Something about our love being viewed
Made me feel exposed, vulnerable and nude
Because amidst the spectacular beauty
The charms of nature unmatched, it's heavy duty

The moonlight washed into our sacred space
Our eyes in harmony trying to trace
The dancing shadows, the smell of mace
But I had the best view, my lovers face

In that moment of pure holy bliss
As we saw each other's souls as we kissed
I pinched myself so hard that I was screaming
But I had to ensure I wasn't dreaming

What is Our Love?

Our love is secret cuddles after sunrise
So as to stay in bed just a little longer
Pretending we're asleep we close our eyes
As Jax's bark for breakfast grows louder and stronger

It is my head on your chest,
Your heartbeat, my breath
No demons troubled my rest
This is the 'Golden Age', I'm Elizabeth

It is your legs wrapped around me
We're on clouds so high
It is you calling me a baby,
Ironic for it's you who is that, I sigh

Love is hot coffee in the morning
Instant will do, what matters is me and you
Yours bitter, mine sweet
And of course Jax waiting for his treat

Love is the sunflowers in their glory
Tall and happy, radiant, proud and affirmatory
It is the garden lush and green
And the birdsong that drowns it, the singers unseen

Love is the joy of a full tummy
Sometimes I'm surprised you found that yummy
Love is the effortlessness of labour
The ingredient that adds all the flavour

Love is the angel descended from heaven
And his jealous bark and silly behavin'
Love is his faith and trust in food
His gentle soul, my life he renewed

Love is the patient, learned wisdom, no violence
Being in the same space even if in silence
It is together growing old and growing wise
As we look at the infinite possibilities in the skies

Love is that peculiar foreshadowing
The peace that comes with our harmonic breathing
That sense of safety and power unfurled
It feels like everything is right in the world

Love is the Guiding Light

Sometimes I feel I'm undeserving of
These bountiful gifts from above
Sometimes I feel I'm unworthy of
This love, in moments I'm not proud of

When in myself I doubt
And nothing can change my mind about
My thoughts a disorganised layout
Timeout, time to sit out

Outside without any possession
My mind is clearer, that's a confession
I can then see my mistaken omission
And make right this life, this mission

While it does beg for patience
And sometimes breeds frustration
If we persevere we will find salvation
Love is the nature of our creation

The mightiest ocean

The most ungodly notion

No matter the station or which nation

The escape will be in devotion

Soft as the feather of a dove

Fitting perfectly like a glove

This is the magic I've dreamed of

This I'd never want to be free of

Sense and sensibility I'm void of

And brain cells I fall short of

But it's you I think of always

Only you I need in this worldly maze

Rising in Love

Not like a torpedo into the ground
Creating an earth-shattering, deafening sound
But like a feather fluttering down
Landing softly as if in a gown
If it landed in water it wouldn't drown
There would be no reason to frown

Falling in itself isn't a fun process
For it entails pain, injury, distress
Applied to love, it could be a mess
Explosions, burnt toast and chess
Do lovers think they need duress?

Real love in truth is like rising
Above the clouds, and further climbing
The sunlight up here is blinding
The fire doesn't burn though, I'm finding
Soaring through the galaxy, deep-diving
Real love doesn't need reminding

To surrender to love is not weaknes
To be vulnerable and real is not bleakness
When really, how lucky are the few
Secure in love to reveal the darkness in you
To be able to be the realest real you

Love is reassuring like fresh morning dew
As the sun's rays burns the mildew
It's an under-appreciated revenue
It is a magic that's meant for two
Never again will Mondays be blue
Falling, then fell, baby I've risen for you

We are Astronauts

Our love spans across the galaxy
And like the galaxy it is expanding still
And expand till the end of time it will

It is brighter than all the stars
That make up the Milky Way
It is every comet in the celestial highway

We are astronauts in spacesuits
Exploring the expanses and discovering
All that there is to loving

When you look up at the night sky
That's us you see in the stars
That's us you see on Mars

And if the Moon is missing from the sky
That's me looking for you
And when I find you she'll be back in view

In the cold space our love is warmth
It is the fire of your embrace
That look on your face

Our love brightens the darkest spaces
Our love is the fusion of all the light
Sunlight, moonlight, starlight, delight

It is a spectacular cosmic casanova
The constellations, every supernova
The exploring will never be over

We are astronauts in space suits
With white overalls and big boots
We are not held down by roots

We Can Fly

We didn't need to leave the city
To see the world

We didn't need to leave home
To experience wonders

The world maybe filled with incredible experiences,
Around the globe fascinating things
But without leaving the bedroom we found wings

Together we can soar through the sky
Together we can fly
Because wonder is you in my eye

And if you lost your wings
I'd search the ends of the earth
Drag them back for your rebirth

Like light years measure distance not time
The longest hours measure nothing
As long as you are mine

Through the travesties of time and space

I will forever look to your embrace

Suddenly the sky doesn't seem so high

Together baby, we can fly

We are Symbiote

You are without question a dreamboat
The lifejacket that keeps me afloat
It's your love that's my source of support
A love that I can only promote

When I'm sick you're the antidote
Our memories a treasured anecdote
A bridge that makes ridiculous the deepest moat
A shield as protective as a royal fort

It's on you alone that I will dote
Joseph in that technicolor dreamcoat
My ship has laid anchor in this port
Who taught you how to court?

But there's something for you to take note
Something that's been at the back of my throat
My love for you isn't a passing boat
For all of time it's for you I cast my vote

For in the storm you are my raincoat

These words be true, I don't sugarcoat

The curve of our love is asymptote

You and I, we are symbiote

Sunday Love

The crooners sing of love on Sundays
A love mature, refined, clear as the sun's rays
The kind of love the defines glory days

A slow love, no explosions
In this we grow, no erosions
The tender kind, in this there is devotion

The love that has weathered the times longer
As steel forged through fire is made stronger
The love that is fulfilling and mature
And seeking elsewhere we don't venture

A love that enjoys the silence
No need for action or violence
The basis of the most loyal alliance
In the face of which there never is defiance

The love that brings us back home
After the world we did roam
Not even the marvels of Rome
Matches the beauty of Sunday love at home

~~Your~~ My Chest

Where we lay our heads at the end of each day
Or from where we long remain on a holiday
The place where we are most at peace I say
Of this place we don't enough parlay

At no place are we more gay
Like the favourite spot of the blue jay
Happy sounds like a baby donkey bray
And yes, donkeys are cute, by the way

While we come to this place from far away
And circle the spot like birds of prey
The lights are off now so it's shadow play
Each night it's action replay

Even if we were in the capital of Paraguay
Which I can't name, neither can I Uruguay
The best doughnuts at San Francisco Bay
Anywhere in the world, that is to say

To this place I have the right of way
So let's get there right away
Where I dream of the Milky Way
Weekend or weekday

It's no joke, no horseplay
This is the shit, it's gourmet
The entree to something risqué
Here there will never be a doomsday

This is the place where everything is ok
Where everyday is a cabaret
When the daylight turns silver-grey
To your chest I ricochet

i love you today

as i will tomorrow and

every day after

Love Gave Me Life

Love is magic and sorcery
It woke something up in me
I was seeing for the first time
I could fly when I called you mine

I don't remember what life was like
Before you entered with that strike
I had been waiting just for you
I had waited in a long queue

I was a creature of the night
With you I liked the morning bright
I wonder if I did even breathe before
With you all of life seems more

Everything suddenly made sense
I actually could appreciate the incense
What was once black or white
For grey you made me want to fight

I could walk, run and fly
Before in bed all day I'd lie
Even in silence I could hear the tune
Aligned like the sun and moon

For you my heart wanted to sing
About the strength you gave my wing
Poetry became involuntary and automatic
Blinding lights in the sky chromatic

Love made me want to give you the world
And roses with their petals whorled
Love showed me beauty and humility
It showered me with peace and serenity

My love for you is infinite
It soars higher than any kite
It gives me the power to take flight
It made living for the first time a delight

your lips on my lips
apocalypse, eyes roll back
it is an eclipse

Voodoo

When I am with you,
Gloomy days have a bright hue
The pain doesn't turn me blue
The devil doesn't get his due

The sorrows that which on any other day
Would beat me down and make me say
"What can I do to make this all go away?"
And helpless in my bed I would lay

All the troubles of the world would be mine
No medication or music would make me fine
I'd resort to goblets of wine
There would be no appetite to dine

My mind would be seeped in melancholy
All attempts to cheer myself up be folly
The dark thoughts in my head, oh golly
My nightmares filled with the creepy crawly

But when I am with you
The demons are no where in view
It does not pain to put on a shoe
I don't need to reach for tissue

How is it that when I am with you
Gone is the cloudy mildew
There is no struggle to push through
What is this lovely voodoo?

you love me though
you haven't seen the best me
i have more in me

The Greatest Gift

Having lost so much of what was me to apathy,
And then on seeing the glass always half-empty,
Always negative intent in ambiguity,
Of feeling at the end of the day empty
The greatest gift you've given me,
Is the ability to once again be me.

you are my sun and

stars i could stare at your face

for infinite hours

Act II: Paradise Lost

you know, i did it
i achieved perfection
it still wasn't enough

The Monstera

Love is the monstera
That's born in darkness but seeks the light
It climbs up the tallest tree with all its might
A glorious, spectacular sight

But it is a blessed compassionate teacher
Evident from its most striking feature
Self-mutilates it's leaves, this creature
So that light penetrates the ground beneath her

About its host tree it does bother
Unlike a fig it doesn't smother
Its roots delicate and careful
They are gentle and so graceful

And if all the stars align
The climate is just perfectly fine
And with the blessings of all that's divine
It will reward you with a delightful fruit along the vine

Just as the power of love is without compare

The monstera fruit is found so rare

Delicious and delightful, it is all that's fair

Dangerous and only for those who dare

But it needs tending, it needs care

It needs protecting even with warfare

The same fruit is toxic if you err

But existing without you my love is a nightmare

Would the toxin at least end the despair?

Fortune Teller

There's a vision of the future I see
A message relayed to the present me
Sent from a potential reality
Of which alternative are many

A harbinger of melancholy I am
At least say I'm consistent, I can
My prophecies have always foretold doom
And I've been right about every fortune

Despite these warnings I hear
Loud and ringing in my ear
Warnings I should indeed fear
I act a fool like King Lear

was it all just an
illusion, our shared love a
lovely delusion?

Alice in Wonderland

My internal controls are distorted
There's a lot therefore misinterpreted
It's a function of my core programming
I wish I was scamming

There's a button that's been turned on
That makes me see negativity
In what is ambiguity
Or even neutrality

These though-loops are not voluntary
They are although quite scary
Riddled with cognitive distortions
Clouded are my observations

I've shared them with you
So you know what plays on my mind
I've learnt to pause when there's a negative view
So that the reality I can find

My internal belief
Which gives me no relief
Is that I can't trust anyone
Because it was family that had me undone

You may see now why
I felt betrayal, abandonment and malice
I didn't ever need to really cry
Because I was in wonderland like Alice

did you fall in love
with your imagination
or the real me

The River in Egypt

The powers that be
Who created the land and sea
Call them gods or demons interchangeably
Hell is real but heaven is make-believe

If omnipotent is what they be
This state of world they want to see
The crimes, injustice and misery
It's for their amusement entirely

They made man in their image
Like 'Sims' but in a world that's sewage
Simple minds believe in bad luck
That about them a god gave a fuck

An existence devoid of meaning
Nothing that's even redeeming
They laugh, they do not cry
As men lived to suffer then die

Cruel tricks they would play
Nefarious I daresay
Give a man hopes and dreams
Celebrating his sorrowful screams

Push a man to the edge
Test what it takes to jump the ledge
Not a test of efficiency
It was cruelty in proficiency

They make man believe in law
Behind which hid a claw
The reward for a good dead
Our pain they celebrated with mead

You say your god is all powerful
Is this life delightful?
Intentional, it was no mistake
A friendly hand, a snake, the stake

Watch my blood engulf the Nile
The price for your ardent denial
You always go the extra mile
I'm glad I was able to make you smile

Addict

When a relationship ends unexpectedly
When it's a shock or surprise
The brain is deprived of oxytocin dramatically
You'll cry even when there's no tears left in your eyes

For the hormones to then return to homeostasis
It can take months or even years
Is that what I'm faced with?
I have enough fears

It wasn't a shock but the impossible
For I didn't for a moment think it's plausible
My whole life I'll be getting over you
Even if you're far from view

Hopeless lovers crave dopamine
Like addicts chase morphine
Even the smallest interaction is a hit
It's a high, I'm an addict

Sometimes

Sometimes I wish I had never known
The life which to me you had shown
A life when I sat upon a golden throne
When dreams infinite I has sown

Perhaps it was all but a dream
To that in agony I scream
Once you and I were a team
A life of strawberries and cream

For living now knowing this
That it was real, a life of bliss
That never again will I have your kiss
For eternity your love I will miss

How do I keep breathing
When this pain so bloody seething?
How do I go on believing
When to this pain there is no relieving?

So sometimes I hate that you

Showed me a life I never knew

So beautiful and kissed with dew

But one I know I can never renew

Grief

Grief is not an empty void
It's not a case of something devoid

It is shouldering the heaviest boulders
Struggling as your body gets older
Not giving up even as the air gets colder
No, because you're a good soldier

It is the suffocation
Empty lungs with no inflation
But breathing still
Breathing with all your will

It is the shattered dreams
Tears that surround me like streams
It is the death of a fantasy
One I desired above all else to see

When gone is that what you call love
No longer feels like the peace of a dove
Hurts like a vengeance powers it
Any light it sees, devours it

In grief our own heart betrays us

It remains beating almost treasonous

Keeps our feet still in that place

So all the pain we have to face

Miseducation

When I learned the theory of pain
I knew but little of it to complain
Thought I had no reference of frame
But pain was my birthname

Learning and then forgetting
Only left then to be regretting
Because we had already unlearned
Just in time to be burned

The nature of the existence
In this universe of pestilence
Where caring is in absence
Do the brave dream of senescence?

Why make a mistake
In things I shouldn't partake
How many times must I learn
These lessons that so painfully burn?

This is a cruel teacher

Torments a lowly creature

The universe opposes my education

And so grips in its hands salvation

Thursday

Today is Thursday.
I had expectations I must say.
That I would be rolling in hay.
That this would be a glorious day
And I would be like the kookaburra gay.

A non-believer I won't pray
So tell me, Sir,
Will I be going 'yay'
or will you be saying 'nay'?

Is it doomsday?
Shall I hideaway?
And as you sashay away
Let my heart decay
Is this another yesterday
Or will we be drinking Chardonnay?

So tell me, ay!
My dreams do not betray
My heart do not lead astray
But if you are to naysay

I plead do not delay
So I may call mayday
For the day then becomes grey

Gem-dear, it is Thursday
What's on the proverbial highway?
In person shall we parlay?
Else heed me don't stay
Walk away
Slip away

Hideaway.
For as I now know with dismay
When you left our shared pathway
Felt a sword though my heart all the way
I felt decomposition underway
But still felt pain in every nerve pathway
I thought that would have gone away
My heart had already turned to sorbet
I was as cold in the ground as Michael Faraday
Electromagnetic radiation couldn't save the day
The call to hell I had to obey
I guess even in death the pain will stay
The Grim Reaper was here to show the way
The path to hell no glorious ballet

Yesterday was that dreadful day
The day the light slipped away
The day the shadows came out to play
For the first time ever did I pray
Told all the gods that any price I'd pay
That my piety would be unmatched from this day
That eternal penance I out lay

When you walked out the doorway
My heart you did fillet
It was the main course and the entree
And the beverage too as it was puree
No need to order take-away

Wasn't it just Valentine's day?
Then with the speed of a railway
Suddenly it was my crucifixion day
It wasn't a dignified display

My heart crushed like paper mache
Over and over I saw it replay
As though cursed by Morgan la Fay
The sorceress from King Arthur's day
Like I was rehearsing a scene for broadway
Would explain the blood-soaked bouquet
I carried on that Ascension Day

How is it that it is Thursday?

When you left did the world not decay?

Didn't the world end like it was doomsday?

Exploded into the Milky Way

And I was thrown onto Hell's Highway?

It was declared the last national holiday,

Because the world ended yesterday

What else would explain the tears of blood I shed that day?

When the world ended and I broke like clay

But how is it another calendar day?

How is it possible it is Thursday?

Sour Flower

I never understood the hype behind flowers
Or why they were exchanged by lovers
Things that only withered by the hour
And did not grant any special power

Butchered appendages of an unlucky organism
Doomed to wither and decay, said my cynicism
Should they have been given a baptism?
For now they called for an exorcism
The bright and beautiful symbolism
Almost mocked my misery and self-antagonism

I created a forest monotoned
My garden was deviod of colour but green
No matter how hard you looked
No other colour would be seen
Only the colour of envy,
My heart was mean
Inert, incapable of valency
Trapped in a dismal tragic fever dream
I did not possess the ability to appreciate beauty
No love, no light; My life and eyes only saw duty

Now my home always has flowers in bloom
Brightening up every corner, every room
They no longer symbolise solitude and doom
And now even in my garden they loom
They exert a strange kind of hypnotism
I could not begin to fathom the mechanism
Something secret shrouded in mysticism
Like a love song in their beauty there is lyricism
It's strange as is the nature of surrealism,
Something so mundane and straightforward,
no euphemism

Now I spot flowers everywhere I go
Surrounding myself with them, I even sow
Garnish my cakes which lifts many an eyebrow
Their beauty lifts my spirits when I am low
Why lovers exchange them I now know

For beauty fends off the shadow
And brightens life like a rainbow
Makes me look forward to tomorrow
Oh, I would not have had this realisation solo
Why did you have to let me go?

Envy & Jealousy

I'll admit I'm envious
Of your world view I'm jealous
I wish I was ignorant too
And see it all as you do

I've seen the worst of humanity
I've seen people's real personality
I saw what people in society
Are truly like in reality

I've learned to spot the fake
The ones who just want to take
Something to validate
Smile but all the while they hate

I've experienced first hand
Abuse and behaviour considered banned
Every trauma in the book
Far I don't have to look

And though you will not lose your position
And not see people transition
You don't see their mission
I tell you naive is your vision

I declare that I do have some authority
After all I studied clinical psychiatry
And there's no place like the hospital
For man's true nature to chronicle

I hope you never have to see
The true face of humanity
And the trust you place in a stranger
Doesn't land you in any danger

But there's worry still
Often you describe someone mentally ill
Praising their duplicity
Not recognizing their toxicity

I wish you'd pay more attention
Look beyond words, see intention
Look inside, what's their motivation
There's a difference between hypervigilence and
paranoid ideation

I know I'm not enough
But I'll admit it's tough
Seeing time you choose to spend
Rather than with me but a friend

It's a double-edged sword, sensitivity
That and emotional maturity
While they aid in empathy
Like a third eye, you can see

Beneath the farce and facade
The unconvincing charade
False masks they parade
As though life was a masquerade

If you should ever truly see
The true nature of humanity
Voluntarily open your eyes
Don't let it be a surprise

But alas, what a twist!
Red flags were sadly missed
Look deeply into the mist
Am I the ugly narcissist?

Trophy

Was it all a fantasy?
Detached and removed from reality?
For I was dreaming of eternity
We'd face the world unitedly
In you I had my family
With you I was safe finally
That you found a soulmate in me
And I loved you so passionately
It happened so suddenly
I'm reeling on the floor emotionally
I'm in unchartered territory
Now I'm anesthetised spinally
My legs are numb lifelessly
How do I survive this catastrophe?
You were my prized trophy

These days

These days are filled with anguish
And all I can do is hope and wish
That you don't in the sea find another fish
A better catch, a tastier dish

I know you said it was over
From those words I can't recover
Felt like being thrown off a tower
Being stripped of all life and power

I'll be just another boy in your past
For me you'd have been the last
One day you'll audition to my role recast
And I'd be praying for my death to come fast

It sounds like its hyperbole
Like, calm down with the rigmarole
But these feeling are real and I can't control
For without you my heart will never be whole

My baggage is too much even to fly first class
So sensitised by trauma I'm made of glass
Get out of my head and touch some grass
If I came to you you'd call it a trespass

This may to you seem like exaggeration
But it's as true as life and creation
For me life is you and your elation
Your elation is from me separation

My existence then so isolate
Sombre, macabre and desolate
Cursing the gods of destiny and fate
On this hallowed ground I commemorate

I look in the mirror and see a raccoon
The skin around my eyes a black-maroon
A caricature of a loony-toon
I pay no heed to the sun or moon

How do I have tears left to cry?
I should by now dehydrate and die
My eyes burn and sting I can't deny
Won't you sing me a lullaby?

Love Isn't What You Think It Is

I'll tell you something that might make you frown
Love is a verb and not a noun
I would never let you drown
I would never let you down

Holiday

Happiness doesn't come from little escapes
To picturesque naturescapes
Because the trouble at home doesn't change
Just because we were out of range

Things fall back into old patterns
As soon as we return from the sojourns
Happiness needs to be built in the permanent place
It needs work to make it a beautiful space

In fact it was always after the return from a holiday
That you would be grim and say
That you had a problem with our relationship
But you had been away from me on a ship

We cannot measure our life by the bubbles
That's surely a formula for troubles
As lovely as the trips maybe
They are not the picture of reality

We should have focussed our time on us
Yes, it was something well worth the fuss
We didn't work on our relationship
And so it become a sinking ship

Lucid

In this moment of lucidity
There's no fog, it's not misty
There's nothing obscuring what I see
In this moment I see clearly

I see you for who you are
I see on myself every scar
You have my heart in a jar
How can I from you be far?

When I spoke up and said
You're messing with my head
On broken glass I tread
Everyday crying in my bed

It was my fault I see now
Back then I didn't see how
I wasn't the real me, I vow
I'll show you the truth somehow

I was going to be with you
My intent you always knew
My inner child frustrated you
That was the only version of me you knew

The child was a child and not grateful
You'll never see me ever again be tearful
To be alone we are so fearful
We had never known a life so delightful

In this moment of lucidity
Alone and afraid my truth I see
I'm working to fix myself voluntarily
It's scary but not too much for me

I won't keep punching at a wall
I won't push myself down and watch myself fall
For intimacy others don't call
I promise you we can have it all

Just come back to me
Just come back, I beg you please
You can have your every release
Together we can be with ease

In this lucid moment I see
Fire engulf the world around me
And in the burning flames I see
A happy you and bleeding me

If you and me was a possibility
I'd move to any forsaken city
I'd ignore the plethora of pity
This is the truth in my lucidity

you don't remember

there was a time you said you'll

love me forever

Pain

I've felt pain before
Even at my core
But it's never been this sour
It hasn't worsened every hour

This pain is so sharp
Cut with strings of a harp
Got to lay down the tarp
Bleeding as if bitten by a shark

I am incapacitated
All limbs amputated
My viscera dissected
And I wasn't sedated

Nothing Hurts Like Heartbreak

I'd die a thousand deaths and more
Even that wouldn't feel so sore
As when you walked out the door
When you said you loved me no more

There was air in my lungs but I couldn't breathe
In my ears the agony a dreadly seethe
Even as I saw the sword unsheath
Standing beneath a cursed wreath

I screamed but no sound was heard
What dismal hell had I incurred?
Forever lonely to be interred
To only look at the mess inward

My heart stopped beating as I held my chest
The pain so sharp but I tried my best
Quite certain I experienced cardiac arrest
By far life's toughest test

But death from heartbreak would be a mercy
And a mercy for me surely a heresy
When my heart was ripped out for all to see
I was still alive watching as demons devoured me

There was a spark once but it left my eye
I suppose that happens if you for days cry
I breathed hard, my most heavy sigh
Did it not pain you to say goodbye?

The floor was ripped from under me
I fell into an endless hole and I couldn't see
Suddenly drowning in the Dead Sea
The tentacles I didn't foresee

The most gruesome confetti
A blood-soaked jubilee
Into my heart was thrust a key
A dagger dipped in poison ivy

My knees buckled and gave way
Fell flat on my face, a segue way
Mouth full of blood I tried to say
Lost my voice but I tried to pray

Never had I experienced such pain
Hurt so hard I was going insane
A downpour of tears as if it was rain
Beating my chest and sobbing in vain

How am I to survive
Having lost the apple of my eye
My Prince with whom my heart lie
I begged for mercy and wished to die

The pain only intensified
Felt as though I was crucified
My soulmate I was denied
A million deaths I died

I plummeted down from up so high
Like Icarus I fell from the sky
The end of my life supply
Soon to fall on spears like a samurai

One Foot in the Past

I blame myself for my past
It keeps stuck, keeps me last
Yesterday I can't look past
Tomorrow's poorly forecast

I don't know how to leg go
In the headlights like a doe
When these are not pleasant things
I hold them close like diamond rings

I live one foot in each realm
One hand grasping each helm
Torn apart as the paths diverge
Crushed as they then converge

I react in the present time
For something that's a past crime
Expecting you to play along
As if you knew the words of the song

I was projecting onto you

Things that were not in view

While this is a common thing to do

I chide myself I did it to you

Why Did My Heart Not Stop

How does my heart go on beating?
It cannot claim ignorance
For in my chest a fire is heating
And my mind is in a trance

The apocalypse came
As did the rapture
Every god and demon you name
And to scavenge came the vulture

The moon ate the sun
While the oceans turned to dust
All of creation had come undone
And my brittle bones began to rust

The sinners were burned
At the stake like witches
The saints heckled them
Were burned, their corpses piled in ditches

The universe engulfed itself
Into a void of nothing
It was the end of all life itself
This is the truth, I'm not bluffing

But why did my heart not stop
When the whole universe did
I wonder this non-stop
Ever since farewell you bid

Sacred

I loved not just you but your body and face
Your body to me was a sacred space
When we touched I felt magic flow through me
I was on earth but heaven I could see

I feel in my stomach a pit
That makes me dizzy I have to sit
When I imagine someone else touching you
When I imagine you with someone new

It feels like a treasure of mine
That I revered as so divine
Something that had become a part of me
Someone else's eyes will see

That what we as holy consecrated
These others have desecrated
For they don't see the value
That I see in you

It feels like a violation

Which is a silly notion

Your body was a scared treasure of mine

These other hands on it feel like a crime

Toughest Battle

Knowing where my soulmate is
But knowing that I will never be his
Keep myself from catching the next flight
This is a damn tough fight

Endless are these nights
Demons give me no respite
In my chest burns a scorching flame
My tears sting like acid rain

How is this pain possible?
How is it even survivable?
Resilience is long gone
This isn't a victory song

At the End

At the end we'll be dead
How much ever in life we get ahead
Doesn't matter what about us was said
Whether we were liked or hated instead
At the end we'll all be dead

And then everything we tired over
Every place that was a layover
Every time we spotted a clover
And those hostile political takeovers
When we're dead there's no voice over

So why all this unnecessary action?
What are we trying to traction?
Our lives we only further fraction
It should be response not reaction
Life without you is putrefaction

A Lesson Too Late

We search and search and search some more
For that one thing that's missing from our lives
That will change everything that was before
That will season food in a special way like chives

We search till the ends of the world
On the highest mountain tops and deepest trenches
For some mystical object to be unfurled
Scorning at time wasted sitting on benches

All the while we have no idea
Not the slightest clue or even a map
A mystery from the times of the Pangea
Some magical thing to unwrap

And as we fail to find it
We don't realise we're wasting time
We fail to see we've fallen into a pit
We don't yet know time lost is a crime

Until one day
In the future long away
We finally sigh and say
To rest this fool's quest we must lay

The years lost and wisdom gained
Finally let us see
There was nothing to be obtained
No reason to search the depths of the sea

That the most precious of things
Are not gold or diamond rings
All the things we had not seen
How foolish we had been

But at least we know now
That while we searched for gold
Invaluable time we have sold
And we are now grey and old

A lesson learned at last
Regretting that we never did cherish
The treasure we have looked past
That we allowed to perish

Life Doesn't Imitate Art

Maybe it was fate
We couldn't even communicate
You were deaf and I was dumb
No wonder the sore thumb

I suppose it wasn't meant to be
If eye-to-eye we couldn't see
Our fundamental beliefs opposed
Differences kept us on our toes
Eachother to do right by
Even in this we didn't comply

A big issue was intimacy
That was shared with others and not me
You wanted past partners in your life
On this we were divided by a knife
I disengaged from mine
For I respected you as divine

There were times I was dramatic
Only because I felt the static
An over-reaction is what you thought
And for that often we fought
Your actions you took logically
While I exploded emotionally

These are differences quite large
For compatibility a large charge
Perhaps we were doomed from the start
You could see that, you are smart
I was fooled by my heart
Thought that life imitated art

No Mercy

You said you wanted out of my life
With words that cut deeper than could a knife
You always did at the slightest strife
I'd wait for your return like a good wife

Each time I was left on the floor bereaved
Cursing love for having me deceived
Your return had me so relieved
For alone I'd otherwise die I believed

I didn't follow the universal rules
Written for me and other fools
My stubbornness matched only by mules
Inside myself were conflicts and duels

I lose all self-control
Panic like I hear a drum-roll
I needed you to be whole
Always the same rigmarole

Don't you know of you I'm so fond?
Don't you feel the unbreakable bond?
I'd swim the ocean and beyond
The universe had me conned

You'd promise to make things right
Fix the things about which we fight
My heart would soar like a kite
But never long lasted the delight

Perhaps this third time's the charm
Because in my head rings the alarm
You no longer bother to charm
You withdraw when I touch your arm

But promises made we never kept
Didn't matter how much I wept
Your plan I could never intercept
The end I had to accept

For though I loved you through it all
When I fell I really did fall
You didn't intend to catch the ball
I had no say, you made the final call

It never took too long
Always a similar song
How did we go so wrong?
Regret I'll carry life long

You always make your exit dramatic
Even in separation you're charismatic
And so once again we fought
To part forever I never thought

When Past & Present Collide

I saw things that weren't there
I saw things that gave me a scare
For I had regressed into a child's mind
And my imagination had run wild

Regression is really true
As real as me and you
When there's past issues unresolved
The inner child to the front is called

When the stars are all misaligned
And the past into the present is reimagined
Familiar feelings like déjà vu
When it happens you don't have a clue

It started with the loss of my voice
Without a voice I had no choice
I lacked the ability of consent
And so back to the past I went

Things only amplified
To cling to the present so hard I tried
But I was vehemently denied
The past was all but personified

The frightful home invasion
I everyday still clearly envision
The man standing so close to me
Threatening to hurt my fur baby

I felt again so unsafe, him so close to my face
So exposed and without mace
I was transported back into my childhood
When I was a little boy who was so good

I've been cut open before
Violated down to my core
In the shadow, behind a closed door
Nearly everyday for 2 years or more

The fear and panic engulfed me
I behaved a child for all to see
I couldn't allow my baby
To be unsafe in childhood like me

So paranoid I became
Even though I thwarted the invaders game
That this home was unsafe I feared
To protect it I up-geared

When the troublesome neighbour called me a child
Amongst other words not so mild
It further took me back in time
Cemented my mind at the site of the crime

I was dissociating and reliving
The worst beyond imagining
Being a child alone and unprotected
Only 7 but already violated

The present me was overwhelmed
The inner child took over the helm
But he did not know how to steer the wheel
He was terrified of everything that wasn't real

He began to act out
For help he even did shout
But even in this body so large
His small voice had no volume charge

This was all too much drama

This childish behaviour not a charmer

The one person in the world who mattered

Walked out the door withered and tattered

just because we had

problems doesn't mean we were

not perfect together

Lately

I feel distant from you lately
Sometimes I think you hate me
We've been there and back again
These days I'm faced with disdain

I talk more and you less
On your phone, I digress
Me and my stories such a bore
To listen to such a chore

I stop midway through
Before the climax was due
You don't realise the silence
What to me feels like violence

You turn your back and fall asleep
While right beside you I sit and weep
I don't wish for life to be fair
But I do wish that you would care

I'm no masochist
Feels like I've been hit by a fist
But an onslaught I endure
Hoping that there's a cure

An antidote for all that's me
That transforms me into something you see
I have the power of invisibility
You'd think in that there's tranquillity

To be with me so much you sacrifice
You remind me as if your heart beat ice
Recite the list of things given up
But that life's an empty cup

As though about them we never spoke
The fights and crying perhaps a joke
The people I'm uncomfortable with
From your past again with them you sit

Salt rubbed into an open wound
Rusty guitar still untuned
I look to you when I am weak
Even then to hurt you seek

I showed you with great pride
A poem I wrote for you and couldn't hide
An unexpected horror ride
When my love for you was denied

While for you everything I reserve
You talk about everything you deserve
As if I'm on trial for heresy
You power up when I beg mercy

Thorny is the crown
Infinite is the drown
When it's me against the whole town
That's when you let me down

Alas this story isn't true
My brain was feeling blue
The child in me was hurting
Desperate for some comforting

But you didn't sign up to babysit
Rightly so, that's a misfit
Doomed by false perceptions
We fell prey to miscommunications

conversation was

all our relationship needed

for it to be saved

Only Love Is Real

This love was unlike any other
I don't wish to have another
All this love and light I found
Remains burning when you aren't around

You were my love and my muse
In your absence it's only blues
I used to pour my overflowing love
Into food and art for you in awe-of

Love taught me to be kind
To be the master of my mind
In everything you I find
If only time I could rewind

I'll love you from afar
You gave me life but with a scar
It will take a lifetime to heal
At least a lifetime that's real

Act III: Tomorrow is a Long Time

Play on My Mind

You play on my mind
When I'm wake and in my dreams
I remember you as generous and kind
Can you hear my agonised screams?

How could I let you go,
When you are my very soul?
How can I let you know,
I'd follow you wherever you may go?

I hear your voice in the breeze
Your soft, loving tone reassuring me
I see your face even in the trees
This version of you has love for me

Not a moment goes by
Whether I look up high
Or close my eyes
Curse up at the skies

You're a part of my soul
Without you I'm not whole
My body aches for your touch
I long for you so much

You're so far removed
I fear I'm doomed
You don't remember the time
You swore you'd be forever mine

I know I'm no swan
But I don't want to move on
I loved you more than you knew
And love you still I do

Love Hurts

Love is an incredible and strange beast
Too formidable to be contained
When it is real and true, it cannot be restrained.

Loving, therefore, an achievement of strength,
A display of valour and guile
The raw power of a crocodile.

It's no surprise therefore,
That an act of such intensity and magnitude
Can to pain, agony and anger allude.

Each time you leave me,
Although I know for certain you will return
I cough out the smoke of heartburn

The dreadful time of separation
Is unlike time of any other situation
It is longer than that of the most accurate calculation

What madness is this

To spend time apart

When time is fleeting and you have my heart?

Alone I'm left to wonder,

Does distance make the heart grow fonder?

How do these lonely days get longer?

Finally, you return to me unfazed,

When we are apart

Do you not feel the pain in your heart?

Each time you came back to me

I believed that I finally had security

The pain of each discard only grew in intensity

Genesis

You took over my existence
Replaced what was once pestilence
Saved me from likely senescence
From hell gave me deliverance

In your absence
You are still my subsistence
Your light still my resonance
No matter the distance

I'm in awe of your intelligence
Of which there's so much evidence
It's not an overemphasis
When I say there was magic in your kiss

There was never any maliciousness
Even in dark times no malevolence
The troubles were in irrelevance
I was showered in benevolence

You were my winged Pegasus

Saved me from a life of recklessness

From partaking in senselessness

From embracing the venomous

It was in your gentleness

In your soft tenderness

I found in myself relevance

I had a rebirth and new genesis

I Dream of a Paradise That I Will Never See

My dreams are a monochrome of green
But it's not envy that is the colour scheme
I dream of forests, plants and trees
With chirping birds and humming bees

I dream of endless plains filled with flowers
And meandering paths meant for lovers
Created by the gods and all their powers
A land where nothing ever sours

Branches heavy with fruit hang low
In the wisdom of the trees is all to know
Gently as the mighty rivers flow
To the grasslands that lie below

The fields kissed by morning dew
The marching ants all in queue
Snow capped mountains just in view
The skies a bright clear blue

Elusive are the creatures crepuscular
Even as the beasts are ripped and muscular
Blink and it's got the prey at the jugular
Of this wild haven I'm the stenographer

Echoing in the dark is the tigers roar
Magnificent power and beauty there could not be more
High up in the sky the birds of prey soar
Harbingers of what's in store

Soon the fields are flooded in moonlight
The stars of the night sky repelled fright
Constellations and comets, what a sight!
The night blooming flowers scent a delight

Orange hues slowly filled the sky
The moon vanished and sun was up high
Spectacular display of colours, I sigh
This beauty none can deny

In the meadows I see the most incredible sight
The one thing I wish for with all my might
The thing I would give everything for
For which any torment I would endure

Happily chasing rabbits in the meadow
Running through the streams that are shallow
His bright grin and loving eyes
He has been my life's prize

I call to him and he runs to me
His wet snout on my cheek is ecstasy
With his glowing halo he's healthy
No diseases weighing him down like in reality

Even his wings have begun to regrow
Those he sacrificed to lessen my sorrow
He's an angel, I always knew
Descended from heaven, didn't I tell you?

But alas, this is all a farce
A good day for him now is scarce
But he's a champion, he soldiers on
For he knows how much on him I depend upon

I dream of a paradise that I will never see
It breaks my heart knowing it will never be
And now even you are gone from my reality
At least for a moment I was happy

I See You

I see you
In every flower and bloom
I feel you
In the house in every room

Sometimes I sit on the couch
And there I can feel your touch
I sit in front of the blank screen of the TV
Wondering if you could see me

I wear the t-shirts you left behind
I can't get you off my mind
I think of you when I'm the tub
How even when wet you'd give me a hug

I miss you when I'm in bed
Your chest where I'd lay my head
Miss the warmth of your embrace
I still see your kind eyes and face

You made this place a home
Where I never thought I'd be alone
We spent the first night together here
You are what makes this place so dear

You are the colour on the walls
You are light when darkness falls
I miss waiting each night for your call
I wrap myself in your shawl

These days I can hardly eat
Still cook for two and with meat
With no spices so I can give the stray
If there's no one else to give away

The pantry still has your snacks
Just looking at them helps me relax
I stare at the door just like Jax
Hoping and praying you'd come back

It is for you that I keep this place
Your memory that is my solace
Every night I sing to you a love song
Knowing it's with you that I belong

Copy Cat

I find myself doing all the things you did
Playing copy-cat like a little kid
Instead of my sweet wine I bought your Riesling
It tasted so much better than that sweet thing

I lie down on the couch for a nap
Any other way to start the day is crap
I make my coffee strong and bitter
I used to make it a whole lot sweeter

I pace up and down the deck
When on a call as I scratch my neck
Trouble Jax with apple slices
He's unamused I'm even copying what he deems vices

Rediscover

How could it be over?
When did things turn sour?
When there's so much left to discover?
I know what was lost we can recover

Perhaps it hasn't yet been our hour
Until forever I will hover
Climb the tallest tower
Not be hindered by any river

I'm now under the darkest cloud cover
The pain is going to boil over
Not every paperback or hardcover
Could describe the beauty of my lover

I will wait undercover
Until we can rediscover
Reclaim the power
Be reunited with my lover

Hope Springs Eternal

Even in darkness
Under trees and canopies
There is that seed that germinates
And while most other seedlings wither away
This one with a resilient and daring heart pushes on
Gathering every bit of strength contained in its leaves
This is as much a test of faith as it is of perseverance
A dream that one day it would see the sky
The glorious sun, constellations
And things unknown
It will be beyond magnificent
The pecking of troublesome birds
Nor trampling over by hooves be its end
The unenviable task at hand was part of the plan

Malnutrition, dehydration, pests that insult creation

Nothing so brilliant and spectacular would come easy

The sun's warm kiss was the coveted prize

Waiting beyond the dense canopy

There were marvels to see

With an unwavering heart

It keeps on marching through the storm

Severed limbs would not be an anchor grounding
Others withered away and perished in their attempt

Sun-seekers that abandoned the quest seethed with envy

For they were resigned to a life in perpetual darkness

Deterred its passionate and humbling endeavour skyward

And soon it pushed its way through the highest trees

And above it was a limitless expanse of sky

No longer stifled and inhaling stale air

The crisp light air without damp

Felt like freedom and ecstasy
This was the stuff of dreams
It actually made it
All the way to the top
Taking the chances of the fools
And trading logic for blind faith
Self-belief and confidence
Carried it to this spot
Where life was always good
And the sun
Oh the sun!
A worthy reward
Everything he had heard was true
But no one had mentioned the magic of light
When only having seen visions hazy in the darkness
For his only frame of reference was sight under the trees

To envision the world clearly with its colour and textures
Seeing the true beauty of the natural world
The hills, the rives, the forests
The birds and the beasts
This was it
This sight was salvation
Enlightenment, wisdom-acquisition
Overwhelming the senses in a seductive way
That he swore that he will from this day always stay
Where light falls and the darkness and shadows retreat
Starved of the fear and insecurity they life leeched-off of
Fear, doubt, uncertainty, these it would never again see
The sights now were the promised lands of legend
That courage, faith, hard-work and bravery
Only possessed by the pure of heart
While the forces of darkness and desolation
Conspire to drain its essence like a vampire would blood
While it did suffer a few cuts and bruises, abuses
The warm rays soothed its tired branches
Soon it was stronger than ever before
Once a sapling, now a mighty tree
It smiled proudly at the sun
It saw the lions run
It had won

The Rose of Jerusalem

Even the tallest trees are torn down
In the mighty storms to the ground
But their roots still cling to the earth
And from this destruction they have rebirth

Just as the birds and the bees
And the fish in all the seven seas
Survive the universe and its oddities
A survival against the odds, no ease

Just as the Jerusalem rose that never dies
Resurrects with the rain from the skies
In time of drought in dormancy it lies
Weather this desiccation so will I

For I know in my heart of hearts
It is foretold in the song and arts
You and I we are destined counterparts
Of one soul we are two parts

if it were up to
destiny and fate our love
would reincarnate

This Love in Me

There's so much love in me
So much I wish you could see
Forever we could live in glee
With me a King you'd be

My only wish in this life
To be your partner, your husband, your wife
But you cut me down with a knife
Expired is my shelf-life

This love in me burns like a passion
Stronger than the will of all creation
More beautiful than all the fashion
It is sincere, kind and with compassion

I always put you above me
My devotion did you not see?
The future glorious that could be
Infinite is this love in me

Wild Flowers

I want to see the wildflowers bloom
On a hillside on a sunny afternoon
The cold breeze on my skin
The fragrance as I breathe in

I want to see the river so blue
I want to see it all with you
Often I wonder if you knew
Just how much I love you

I was yours and you were mine
The tallest mountain an easy climb
This was undoubtedly holy, divine
We were a happy family for a time

Perfect

We weren't perfect when we met
Wouldn't that have been a boring set
We had the chance to grow together
We didn't even really know each other

You could have leaned on me
I'd have stayed no matter the degree
I'd have shared your troubles and burdens
Never left your side when you were hurtin'

Together we could help each other heal
Alone we wouldn't need to deal
With the pains of the past that are so real
This life which is a roulette wheel

Perfection has been my life's quest
Always tried hard but failed every test
You've seen with your own eyes
My attempts, my failure and heard my cries

We don't need to be perfect
Don't need all the boxes checked
It's alright to have a defect
As long as on it we reflect

What matters is that we recognise
The things that we need to revise
Together we can fight for each other
We can attain perfection together

Run to You

All I want to do
Is run to you
I wish you knew
How much I loved you

But even if I flew to you
Our love would not grow anew
There's no love left for me in you
You'd rather be with someone new

I'd do anything to go back in time
The Universe took what was mine
I'd make it pay for that crime
If only there was a chance you'd be mine

You said there was nothing left
All your love for me bereft
Words that felt to my heart like theft
Broke in pieces along the cleft

I'd run to the moon, Jupiter, Neptune
Barefoot over scorching sand dune
If I had a chance with you
There's nothing I wouldn't do

I'd run under the blazing sun
Even as a vampire that would be undone
I'd run to hell if I had too
I'd run anywhere for you

Television

For the first time in years
I decided to face my fears
Alone I turned on the TV
Although afraid of what I'd see

Trigger-happy I had become
My past unable to overcome
Ready to fire like a loaded gun
Irked by everything under the sun

I was afraid of the subliminal things
Jokes others would find amusing
The comedies were always most scarring
With their jabs at intimate violence most jarring

With you I felt safe
I was no longer that forsaken waif
I could stand up to the fear that ruled me
Which told me I was weak and fooled me

In the time that you've been gone
The inner voice with vengeance was reborn
Sleep came only after sunrise
Waiting for another invader I'd never close my eyes

But today because of you
I felt ready to change my view
I struggled with the remote
You'd have laughed yourself out of your coat

But I did finally persevere
My only virtue you'll hear
I watched Poirot as though you were here
And I felt as if you were near

I barely paid attention to be honest
You know, I kept every promise
For the first time since you walked out the door
The tears on my face weren't a sad score

Gravity

This pain is like a white light
So sharp and so bright
Ironic that even with my medical degree
All I can do is endure the autophagy

Is it a consequence of consciousness
My thoughts are in incontinence
Everything seems ominous
This trench is bottomless

Gravity is supposed to hold things to the ground
It makes the rain fall down
But not all the water goes to the ocean
Some of it goes into clouds for recreation

But there's things that defy gravity
And I don't mean the birds and bees
In the battle against gravity something has won
For fire goes up and points to the sun

All things strive for their source

For anything else is a life of remorse

I don't fear the power of gravity

It can't keep you from me

Lucid Delusions

There's an aspect of delusion
When love isn't a union
You can't help hoping your love will be returned
Even when you have been spurned

Loving is all-consuming
Unseparate from the self, like breathing
And just as not breathing is not an option
To stay alive loving feels a necessary action

The body fights back as if you were drowning
A survival instinct that's default programming
For a beating heart is a prerequisite to live
'Love' and 'live' are corroborative

If breathing was voluntary
Sleep would mean the cemetery
Which is what it also feels like to me
Like what life without love would be

It's an impossible effort
Body and mind in discomfort
To convince your body to stop opposing
Something it believes to be life-sustaining

Hope is a wicked thing
For it is from where the delusions spring
You can try and fight it with logic
But results are gonna be tragic

Because being in love by definition
Includes an uncontrollable ideation
That which is the fault of hope
Which has you daydreaming like life's a soap

There's no disentangling the desire
It's like removing flame from fire
Inherently an impossible task
That which of me is asked

Until the day I no longer love you
Which when 'love is life' is my view
Is a thought that I can't compute
Painful like a screeching flute

For the sake of discussion
I'll resolve to the hypothetical construction
That love isn't a conditional factor for life
That its removal isn't to the heart a knife

And within this theoretical frame
Life can be played like a game
And I'll cease from loving you
But not cease from existence too

I try with great effort to convince myself
To see the truth for what it is
That it's blatant stupidity
To pine over one who doesn't love me

It seems bitter-sweet
This scary and daunting feat
Because until then I suffer the constant pain
Of rejection every second that drives me insane

If you haven't figured of what I speak
What intangible force makes me weak
Is that love to me is returned
That my delusional dreams are not burned

the moon vanishes
only to return stronger
so shall I return